Do You KNOW?

Your WIFE

by Dan Carlinsky

 sourcebooks

Published by Sourcebooks, Inc.
P.O. Box 4410, Naperville, Illinois 60567-4410
(630) 961-3900
FAX: (630) 961-2168
www.sourcebooks.com

Library of Congress Cataloging-in-Publication Data

Carlinsky, Dan.
  Do you know your wife? / by Dan Carlinsky.
    p. cm.
  (alk. paper)
  1. Women. 2. Man-woman relationships. I. Title.
  HQ801 .C27755 2004
  305.4—dc22
                              2003020059

Printed and bound in China

OGP 30 29 28 27 26 25 24 23 22 21 20

Think you know all about the woman on the other side of the dinner table? Well, maybe. Let this little book be the judge.

The fact is, no matter how long you've been together, there's probably plenty you don't know about the woman in your life. If the two of you are like most couples, you probably talk more about the neighbors and the news than about yourselves. The result: an information gap.

Counselors say that knowing about your partner's past and preferences can be important—even things like "Who was her best friend in grade school?" and "Does she hate squash?" Knowing, they say—even knowing such bits of trivia—is a sign of caring.

Now, that's not to say that if you and she are on the verge of a split, knowing her shoe size will save your relationship. But, as the lady said as she offered chicken soup to the dying man, "It couldn't hurt!"

So grab a pencil and show what you know. The answers, of course, are not in the book; only she can say. So after you've completed the test, ask her to check your answers and figure your score.

The test has 100 questions. Count ten points for each correct answer. Where you miss some of a multi-part question, divide and take partial credit; you'll need all the help you can get. Here's how to rate yourself:

Above 900: Very impressive. In fact, downright amazing.

700-900: Pretty good, but you might want to work a little to polish off your knowledge. Start asking questions...and pay attention.

Below 700: Weak. Ask her to give you a remedial course.

Take the "Do You Know Your Wife?" test. You may find you have something to brag about, or you may be humbled. Either way, just by going over your answers together, you'll learn a little and have some fun as well. Good luck.

—D.C.

1. FOR STARTERS, WILL SHE TAKE THIS TEST:

_____ Eagerly?

_____ Indifferently?

_____ Kicking and screaming?

2. SHE USUALLY CARRIES ENOUGH CASH TO:

_____ Buy a cup of coffee

_____ Cover lunch for herself

_____ Treat a crowd to dinner and then some

3. WHEN SHE HAS A HEADACHE SHE USUALLY TAKES:

_____ An aspirin

_____ Two aspirin

_____ Another pain medication

_____ Nothing

4. DID SHE EVER WIN A CONTEST OF ANY SORT? IF SO, WHAT WAS HER PRIZE?

_____ Yes, she won _____

_____ No

5. WHAT'S HER FAVORITE COLOR?

_____

6. WHEN DRESSING FOR AN EVENING OUT, DOES SHE PUT ON MAKEUP:

_____ Early in the process?

_____ Last thing?

_____ Not at all?

7. WITHIN TWO, HOW MANY KEYS DOES SHE CARRY?

_____

8. WHICH SHIRT OF YOURS DOES SHE REALLY LIKE?

_____

9. IF YOU WANT TO MAKE HER UNHAPPY, SERVE HER

_____ FOR DINNER.

10. WHO'S HER FAVORITE SINGER?

_____

11. HOW OFTEN DOES SHE GENERALLY SHOP FOR GROCERIES?

_____ Once a week or less

_____ Twice a week

_____ Three times a week or more

12. IF HER BEST FRIEND PASSED ALONG A JUICY PIECE OF GOSSIP AND WARNED HER NOT TO TELL A SOUL, WOULD SHE TELL YOU?

_____ Absolutely not

_____ She might

_____ She probably would

_____ Of course

13. WHAT WAS HER TELEPHONE NUMBER WHEN YOU FIRST MET?

_____

14. WHEN SHE WAS A LITTLE GIRL, WHAT DID SHE ANSWER PEOPLE WHO ASKED, "WHAT DO YOU WANT TO BE WHEN YOU GROW UP?"

_____

16. HAS SHE KEPT ANY OBJECT—A BOOK, A TOY, A DOLL—SINCE CHILDHOOD?

_____ Yes, _____

_____ No

15. IF SHE HAD A CHANCE TO HAVE HER FORTUNE TOLD FOR FREE, WOULD SHE:

_____ Accept and heed the fortune teller's words?

_____ Accept but treat the whole thing as a joke?

_____ Decline because she thinks such stuff is nonsense?

17. IT'S LATE AT NIGHT. THE PHONE RINGS. SHE ANSWERS AND HEARS HEAVY BREATHING, THEN A STRING OF OBSCENITIES. WHAT DOES SHE DO?

_____ Panic

_____ Hang up and go back to sleep

_____ Keep listening

_____ Yell at the caller

_____ Laugh

_____ Hand the receiver to you

18. HOW OLD WAS SHE ON HER FIRST DATE?

_____

19. WHEN SHE COMES HOME TO AN EMPTY HOUSE, DOES SHE IMMEDIATELY TURN ON A RADIO OR TELEVISION?

_____ Yes

_____ No

20. DO YOU KNOW HER FEET? CHECK THE APPROPRIATE LINE.

_____ Her left foot is slightly larger than her right

_____ Her right foot is slightly larger than her left

_____ As far as she can tell, they're the same size

21. IF THE WASHING MACHINE BROKE DOWN, WHAT WOULD SHE DO?

_____ Try to fix it

_____ Call a repairman

_____ Call you

_____ Wait until you got home

22. AT A PICNIC, WOULD SHE RATHER DRINK:

_____ Beer?

_____ White wine?

_____ Red wine?

_____ Iced tea?

_____ Soft drink?

23. HAS SHE EVER BOUGHT A LOTTERY TICKET?

_____ Yes

_____ No

24. WHAT'S HER FAVORITE CLOTHING OR DEPARTMENT STORE?

_____

25. DOES SHE WEIGH HERSELF AT LEAST ONCE A WEEK?

_____ Yes

_____ No

26. IF YOU WANTED TO SURPRISE HER BY MAKING RESERVATIONS AT HER FAVORITE RESTAURANT, WHICH PLACE SHOULD YOU CALL?

_____

27. APPROXIMATELY HOW MANY NOVELS HAS SHE READ IN THE PAST YEAR?

_____ None

_____ One

_____ Two to five

_____ More than five

28. DOES SHE EVER READ COOKBOOKS JUST FOR FUN?

_____ Yes

_____ No

29. DOES SHE EVER INVENT HER OWN RECIPES?

_____ Often

_____ Sometimes

_____ Never

30. WHAT'S HER MOTHER'S MAIDEN NAME?

_____

31. WHAT'S HER PARENTS' STREET ADDRESS?

_____

32. IF SHE'S SERVED CHICKEN, SHE'LL REACH FIRST FOR:

_____ White meat

_____ Dark meat

_____ Either

_____ Something other than chicken

33. WHAT PIECE OF FURNITURE—IN ANY ROOM—WOULD SHE MOST LIKE TO REPLACE?

_____

34. DOES SHE KEEP A PHOTO OF YOU:

_____ In her wallet?

_____ At work?

35. WHO WAS HER FAVORITE BEATLE?

_____ John

_____ Paul

_____ George

_____ Ringo

_____ Favorite what?

36. HAS SHE EVER USED A POWER SAW?

_____ Yes

_____ No

37. IF YOU TWO HAD TO MOVE OUT OF THE COUNTRY, WHERE WOULD SHE CHOOSE TO GO?

_____

38. WHAT'S THE ONE TELEVISION PROGRAM SHE CAN'T DO WITHOUT?

_____

39. IF A VOLUNTEER FROM A CHARITY KNOCKED ON THE DOOR AND ASKED FOR A CONTRIBUTION, WHAT WOULD SHE DO?

_____ Make a token gift

_____ Give more

_____ Politely decline to give

_____ Rudely say no

40. WHAT COLOR IS HER EVERYDAY HANDBAG?

_____

41. DID SHE HAVE A TV IN HER BEDROOM WHEN SHE WAS A KID?

_____ Yes

_____ No

42. GIVEN A WELL-STOCKED FRUIT BOWL, WHICH WOULD SHE MOST LIKELY CHOOSE FIRST?

_____ Apple

_____ Banana

_____ Orange

_____ Grapes

_____ Pear

_____ None — she'd look for a doughnut

43. WHAT WOULD SHE SAY ABOUT THE IDEA OF A STRIP CLUB A MILE FROM YOUR HOME?

_____ "Where do I sign to protest?"

_____ "Makes no difference to me."

_____ "Great!"

_____ "Hmm. I wonder if they're hiring."

45. WOULD SHE DONATE A KIDNEY TO:

_____ A close relative?

_____ A close friend?

_____ You?

44. WHEN SHE PASSES A MIRROR OUTSIDE THE HOUSE, WHAT DOES SHE USUALLY DO?

_____ Glance at her reflection and keep walking

_____ Stop and inspect herself very carefully

_____ Ignore the glass and go on her way

46. WHICH WOULD SHE RATHER DO?

____ Wash dishes

____ Dry dishes

47. WHICH WOULD SHE PREFER?

____ A full-time maid

____ A full-time cook

____ Neither (honestly)

48. DOES SHE KNOW WHO PYTHAGORAS WAS?

____ Yes

____ No

49. HOW OFTEN DOES SHE WASH HER HAIR?

____ Daily

____ Every other day

____ Twice a week

____ No more than weekly

50. WHAT'S HER FAVORITE FLOWER? (FIVE BONUS POINTS IF YOU KNOW THE COLOR TOO.)

_____

51. WHERE WOULD SHE RATHER VACATION?

_____ In a private mountain cabin with a fireplace

_____ At a beach resort

_____ Any place with good shopping

52. WHAT JEWELRY DOES SHE WEAR JUST HANGING OUT AT HOME?

_____ Engagement ring

_____ Wedding band

_____ Other ring(s)

_____ Bracelet(s)

_____ Earrings

_____ Anything else

55. DOES SHE THINK MOST STANDUP COMICS ARE FUNNY?

_____ Yes

_____ No

_____ Sort of

53. HOW DOES SHE LIKE MOST MEAT?

_____ Rare

_____ Medium rare

_____ Medium

_____ Medium well

_____ Well done

_____ She doesn't

54. NAME AT LEAST TWO OF HER OLD TEACHERS. (ANY GRADE WILL DO.)

_____

56. WHICH SECTION OF A NEWSPAPER IS SHE MOST LIKELY TO READ FIRST?

_____

57. HOW MANY CREDIT AND CHARGE CARDS DOES SHE CARRY?

_____ None

_____ One to three

_____ Four to six

_____ More

58. DOES SHE CLOSE THE BATHROOM DOOR WHEN NO ONE ELSE IS HOME?

_____ Yes

_____ No

59. DOES SHE KNOW THE FIRST NAMES OF AT LEAST TWO OF HER GREAT-GRANDPARENTS?

_____ Yes

_____ No

60. WHEN SHOPPING FOR CLOTHES, DOES SHE PREFER:

_____ To browse and ask questions only when necessary?

_____ To be helped by a salesperson from the start?

61. CAN SHE NAME A CURRENTLY ACTIVE PROFESSIONAL:

_____ Golfer?

_____ Tennis player?

_____ Jockey?

62. DOES SHE KNOW THE CAPITAL OF ARGENTINA?

_____ Yes

_____ No

63. WILL SHE KNOW HOW MANY MILES IN 100 KILOMETERS?

_____ Yes

_____ No

64. CAN SHE NAME ANY PAINTING BY PABLO PICASSO?

_____ Yes

_____ No

65. WHEN WAS SHE AT HER LIFETIME HIGH WEIGHT? (OR IS SHE AT HER HEAVIEST RIGHT NOW?)

_____

66. IF OFFERED SOME CHOCOLATE-COVERED TERMITES AS A "DELICACY," SHE WOULD:

_____ Try some out of genuine interest

_____ Try some to be polite

_____ Gently decline, explaining that the thought doesn't appeal to her

_____ Make up an excuse like "Sorry, I'm dieting"

67. IF SHE SAW ONE OF HER FAVORITE MOVIE ACTORS ON THE STREET, ALONE, WOULD SHE:

_____ Pretend she didn't notice him?

_____ Nod or say hello and keep walking?

_____ Politely ask for his autograph and leave?

_____ Try to engage him in conversation?

68. IF SHE DEVELOPED A TERMINAL ILLNESS, WOULD SHE:

_____ Want to know in detail?

_____ Want to know just the basics?

_____ Prefer not to be told?

69. IN WHICH FINANCIAL CATEGORY WOULD SHE PLACE HER FAMILY WHEN SHE WAS GROWING UP?

_____ Rich

_____ Comfortable

_____ Just managing

_____ Really struggling

70. DID SHE HAVE A CHILDHOOD NICKNAME?

_____ Yes, the kids called her _____

_____ No

71. IF SHE COULD NAME HER JOB, WHAT WOULD SHE WANT TO DO?

_____

72. HOW DOES SHE USE SALT AT THE TABLE?

_____ Adds it to some foods even before tasting

_____ Adds it only after tasting

_____ Rarely or never uses it

73. WHICH OF THESE CAN'T SHE DO?

_____ Touch her toes

_____ Stand on her head

_____ Jumpstart a car

_____ Rewire a lamp

74. WHICH STATEMENT BEST EXPRESSES HER THINKING?

_____ "Most women are better off married"

_____ "Most women are better off single"

_____ She wouldn't make either blanket statement

75. SHE ALWAYS CARRIES WITH HER:

_____ A list of phone numbers

_____ A safety pin

_____ Tissues

_____ Something to eat

_____ Drinking water

76. WHAT'S HER FAVORITE HOLIDAY?

_____

77. DOES SHE HAVE ANY MAJOR REGRETS IN HER LIFE THAT ARE FREQUENTLY ON HER MIND?

_____ Yes, _____

_____ No

78. SHE USUALLY FALLS ASLEEP:

_____ As soon as her head hits the pillow

_____ Within a few minutes

_____ With great difficulty

79. IF SHE WENT AWAY FOR SEVERAL DAYS AND RETURNED TO FIND THAT YOU HAD MADE A DRAMATIC CHANGE IN YOUR APPEARANCE (YOU GREW A BEARD, YOU DYED YOUR HAIR), WHAT WOULD SHE MOST LIKELY DO?

_____ Complain that you didn't consult her

_____ Compliment you

_____ Laugh

80. "THERE'S NOTHING WRONG WITH SEPARATE VACATIONS. IN FACT, IT'S NOT A BAD IDEA AT ALL." WILL SHE:

_____ Agree?

_____ Disagree?

81. IF SHE CAME INTO A LOT OF MONEY, IN WHAT ORDER WOULD SHE RANK THESE POSSIBLE USES FOR THE CASH?

_____ Debts

_____ Dream purchases

_____ Family

_____ Friends

_____ Charities

82. WITHOUT LOOKING, TELL HOW SHE PARTS HER HAIR.

_____ On the left

_____ On the right

_____ In the center

_____ Not at all

83. WOULD SHE RATHER BE BURIED OR CREMATED?

_____ Buried

_____ Cremated

_____ No opinion

84. DOES SHE OWN A BLUE COAT?

_____ Yes

_____ No

85. WHEN DID SHE MOST RECENTLY CHEW BUBBLE GUM?

_____ Very recently

_____ Within the past year or so

_____ A few years back

_____ Many years ago, if ever

86. DOES SHE DOODLE WHILE TALKING ON THE TELEPHONE?

_____ Often

_____ Sometimes

_____ Never

87. HOW MANY CUPS OF COFFEE OR TEA DOES SHE DRINK IN A TYPICAL DAY?

_____ None

_____ One to three

_____ Four to six

_____ Seven or more

91. WHEN SHE GETS SOMETHING NEW, DOES SHE GENERALLY:

_____ Use it right away?

_____ Save it "for best"?

88. IF, FOR SOME REASON, YOU TWO HAD TO ATTEND AN HOUR-LONG MUSICAL SKIT PERFORMED BY A GROUP OF CHILDREN, NOT ONE OF THEM RELATED TO YOU, WOULD SHE:

_____ Enjoy herself?

_____ Tolerate the show?

_____ Claw at the seat until the thing was over?

89. IS THERE ANYTHING YOU CAN DO THAT SHE CAN'T, THAT SHE'D LIKE YOU TO TEACH HER?

_____ Yes, _____

_____ No

90. OF HER MARRIED WOMEN FRIENDS, WHO DOES SHE THINK PICKED THE BEST HUSBAND?

_____

92. "A PERSON WITH HEALTHY EYES WHO WEARS DARK GLASSES
INDOORS IS EITHER PRETENTIOUS OR A LITTLE CRAZY."
WOULD SHE:

_____ Agree?

_____ Disagree?

_____ Decline to give a simple yes or no?

_____ Have no opinion?

93. HAS SHE BOUGHT ANYTHING BY MAIL ORDER OR FROM A
TELEVISION SHOPPING SHOW WITHIN THE PAST YEAR?

_____ Yes

_____ No

94. DOES SHE BELIEVE IN A PERSONAL GOD WHO INTERVENES IN
HUMAN AFFAIRS?

_____ Yes

_____ No

_____ She can't say

95. DOES SHE HAVE A FAVORITE PERFUME?

_____ Yes, _____

_____ No

96. WHICH COLOR OR COLORS DOES SHE THINK YOU LOOK BEST IN?

_____

97. CAN SHE SING HER OLD SCHOOL SONG?

_____ Yes

_____ No, but she can hum the tune

_____ She can't remember it at all

98. CAN SHE NAME THE CURRENT SECRETARY GENERAL
OF THE UNITED NATIONS?

_____ Yes, easily

_____ Yes, after some thought

_____ She'll come close

_____ No way

99. IF SHE WERE GOING TO GET A NEW PET TOMORROW, WHAT
KIND OF ANIMAL WOULD SHE WANT? AND WHAT BREED?

_____

100. WHAT'S HER FAVORITE MOVIE OF THE PAST FIVE YEARS?

_____

WHAT <u>DON'T</u> YOU KNOW ABOUT HIM?

$5.95 U.S./$7.95 CAN/£3.99 UK • 978-1-4022-0199-8
Available at your local bookstore or by calling (800) 727-8866.